The story of:

_____

*Grandparents
are the footsteps to
future generations.*

AUTHOR UNKNOWN

Scripture quotations are taken from the Holy Bible, New International Version®, NIV®. Copyright © 1973, 1978, 1984, 2011 by Biblica, Inc.® Used by permission. All rights reserved worldwide; and from the New King James Version®. Copyright © 1982 by Thomas Nelson, Inc. Used by permission. All rights reserved.

Papercut Artwork © 2017 by Ginger Chen
Cover and interior design by Nicole Dougherty

TO MY GRANDKID

Copyright © 2018 by Harvest House Publishers
Published by Harvest House Publishers
Eugene, Oregon 97408
www.harvesthousepublishers.com

ISBN 978-0-7369-7284-0

Printed in China

18 19 20 21 22 23 24 25 26 / RDS-ND / 10 9 8 7 6 5 4 3 2 1

To My Grandkid

HARVEST HOUSE PUBLISHERS
EUGENE, OREGON

Being a grandparent is an unparalleled experience.

You get to hold chubby babies, chase mischievous toddlers, teach curious preschoolers…spoil, love, pray, repeat. You have an opportunity to see your legacy living out in your grandchildren. A more incredible blessing is hard to imagine.

You would do anything for your grandkid, wouldn't you? Do you know you have a story to share? That is something your grandchild will cherish. This book will help you capture snippets of your unique life story as you write them down and then share them in this gift to your grandkid.

Don't worry about completing this book within a specific time frame. Open it when you can, when you are thinking about it. It's meant to be simple—and yet more meaningful than you can imagine.

My Childhood

My Career

Love & Marriage

Parenting

About Me

Wisdom

You & Me!

Let the little children come to me and do not hinder them, for the kingdom of heaven belongs to such as these.

THE BOOK OF MATTHEW

My Childhood

Our
Family Tree

Great-Grandma

Great-Grandpa

Grandma

Great-Grandma

Great-Grandpa

Grandpa

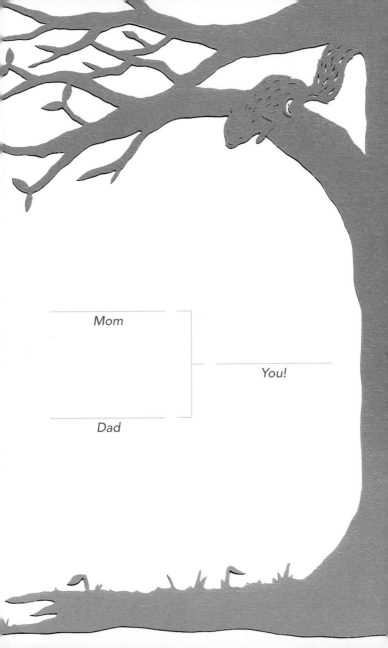

Mom

Dad

You!

My Birthday

I was born on

_____ / _____ / _____ at _____

I was born in

_____

I weighed

_____ lbs. & _____ oz.

My whole name is

_____

My parents almost named me

_____

My favorite memory of my mom is

My favorite memory of my dad is

My favorite subject(s) in school were

_____

_____

_____

My favorite teacher in school was

_____

because _____

_____

_____

_____

_____

_____

_____

_____

_____

_____

_____

_____

_____

I participated in these sports or activities.

My favorite vacation was

because

My favorite birthday growing up was

_____

_____

_____

_____

_____

_____

_____

My favorite birthday as an adult was

As a kid, my family Christmas traditions included

Here are some of the lyrics to
my favorite song as a teenager.

_____

_____

_____

_____

_____

_____

_____

_____

_____

_____

_____

_____

As a kid, my room was covered in posters of (or decorated with)

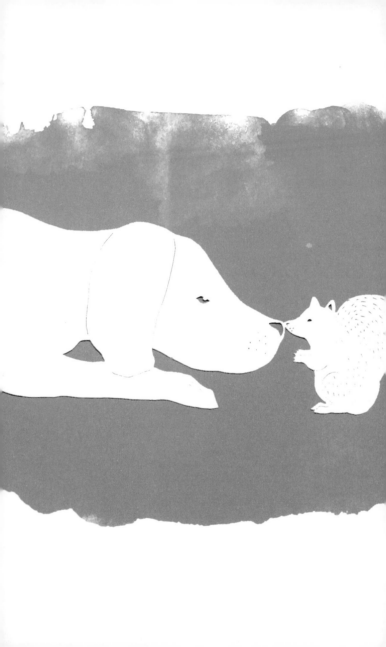

The name of my first pet was

_____

He / **She** was a

_____

_____

_____

I landed this part in the school play.

_____

_____

_____

Something memorable
that happened was

The funniest thing I did as a kid was

_____

_____

_____

_____

_____

_____

_____

_____

The scariest thing that
happened to me as a kid was

When I was a kid,
my grandma and I would

_____

_____

_____

_____

_____

_____

_____

_____

_____

_____

_____

_____

_____

When I was a kid,
my grandpa and I would

_____

_____

_____

_____

_____

_____

_____

_____

_____

_____

_____

_____

_____

My first...

Word

Toy

Food

Memory

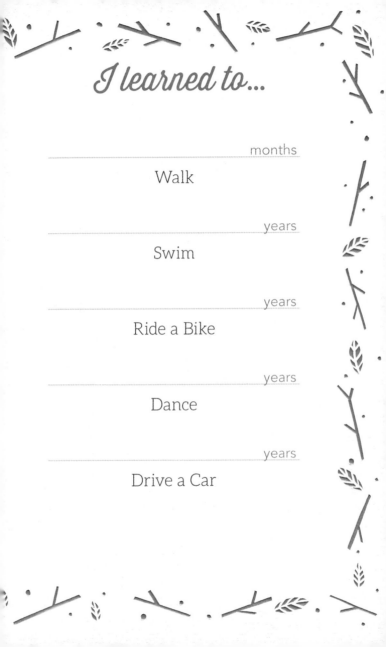

I learned to...

_____ months

Walk

_____ years

Swim

_____ years

Ride a Bike

_____ years

Dance

_____ years

Drive a Car

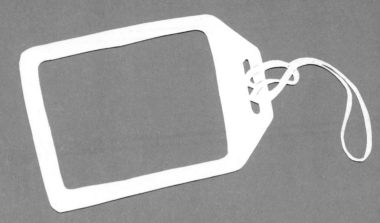

My nickname(s) were

_____

_____

_____

The story is

_____

_____

_____

_____

_____

_____

_____

_____

_____

_____

_____

_____

_____

_____

_____

_____

_____

_____

_____

My first car was

_____

A gallon of gas at that time cost

$ _____

My dream car is

_____

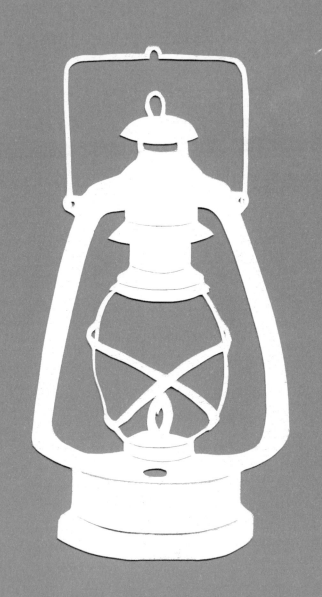

I graduated from

_____ High School.

There were _____ students
in my graduating class.

I **did** / **didn't** go to college.

Here's what I learned.

_____

_____

_____

_____

_____

_____

You won't believe it, but

_____

wasn't even invented when I was kid.

Instead, we used _____

_____

_____

_____

_____

_____

_____

_____

_____

_____

My best friends were

_____

_____

_____

_____

_____

When I was growing up,
my friends and I would

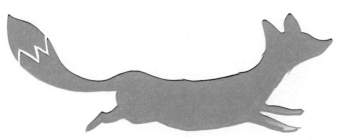

When I was younger, I enjoyed

And now that I'm older, I still enjoy

The most important lesson
I learned as a kid was

*Whatever you do,
work at it with all your heart,
as working for the Lord.*

THE BOOK OF COLOSSIANS

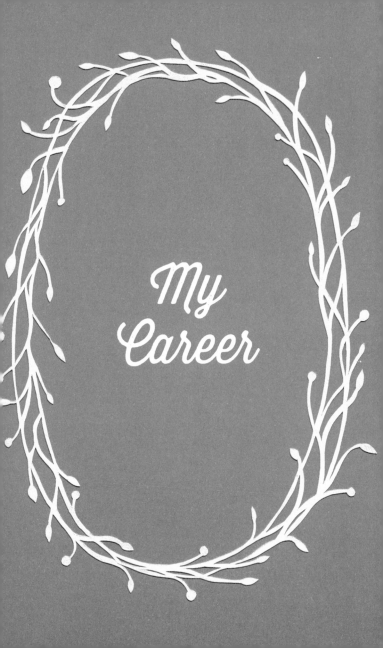

My
Career

When I was a kid, when
I grew up I wanted to be

It **did** / **didn't** happen, and I'm

glad / **sad** / **relieved** / **still doing it.**

When I was growing up,
my parents' jobs were

_____

_____

_____

My first job was as a

_____

I was paid

$ _____

My job duties included

_____

_____

_____

_____

_____

_____

My favorite job was

_____

_____

I loved it because

_____

_____

_____

_____

_____

_____

_____

_____

_____

_____

_____

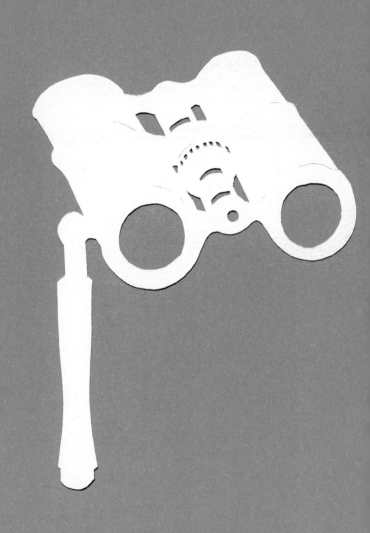

The biggest impact I've
had in my career was

Love...

bears all things,
believes all things,
hopes all things,
endures all things.
Love never fails.

THE BOOK OF 1 CORINTHIANS

Love &
Marriage

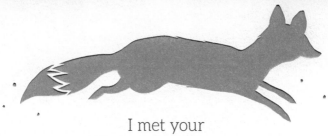

I met your
grandma / **grandpa**

My favorite thing about
Grandma / **Grandpa** is

Here's the story of our first date.

_____

_____

_____

_____

_____

_____

_____

_____

_____

_____

_____

_____

_____

Here is the story of our engagement.

_____

_____

_____

_____

_____

_____

_____

_____

_____

_____

_____

We were married

_____ / _____ / _____
Date

_____
Place

_____

_____

_____
Colors

A favorite memory from the day was

For this child I prayed.

THE BOOK OF FIRST SAMUEL

Parenting

Your **mom** / **dad** was born

_____ / _____ / _____
Date

_____
Place

_____
Time

_____
Weight

_____
Hair Color

_____
Eye Color

I had _____ *kids.*

Their names and birthdays are

_____

_____ / _____ / _____

_____

_____ / _____ / _____

_____

_____ / _____ / _____

_____

_____ / _____ / _____

_____

_____ / _____ / _____

_____

_____ / _____ / _____

_____

_____ / _____ / _____

Your **mom** / **dad** was
like this as a kid.

Here's one of my favorite memories
of your **mom** / **dad** as a kid.

You remind me of your
mom / **dad** in these ways.

Here's an embarrassing story
about your **mom** / **dad**.

_____
_____
_____
_____
_____
_____
_____
_____
_____
_____
_____
_____
_____
_____
_____
_____
_____

Our favorite thing to do as a family was

_____

_____

_____

_____

_____

_____

_____

_____

_____

Other family traditions included

_____

_____

_____

_____

_____

_____

_____

_____

_____

_____

_____

_____

_____

_____

_____

_____

We are His workmanship, created in Christ Jesus for good works, which God prepared beforehand that we should walk in them.

THE BOOK OF EPHESIANS

About Me

I've checked off these things on my bucket list.

- ☑ _____
- ☑ _____
- ☑ _____
- ☑ _____
- ☑ _____
- ☑ _____
- ☑ _____
- ☑ _____
- ☑ _____
- ☑ _____
- ☑ _____
- ☑ _____
- ☑ _____
- ☑ _____
- ☑ _____

I've yet to check off these things
on my list.

☐ _____

☐ _____

☐ _____

☐ _____

☐ _____

☐ _____

☐ _____

☐ _____

☐ _____

☐ _____

☐ _____

☐ _____

☐ _____

☐ _____

☐ _____

My Favorites

Color

Food

Dessert

Song

Hymn

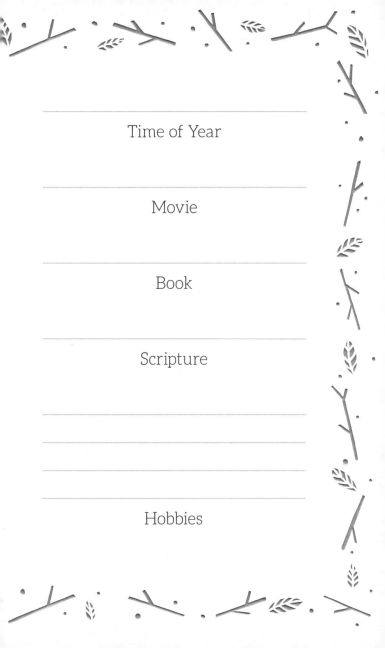

Time of Year

Movie

Book

Scripture

Hobbies

My top five favorite candy bars are

1. _____

2. _____

3. _____

4. _____

5. _____

*In case you want to bring me
one of each when you visit.*

Here's a little something crazy
about me I've never told you.

Every time I

I thank God and smile.

My Favorite Meal

Ingredients:

_____
_____
_____
_____
_____

Directions:

_____
_____
_____
_____
_____
_____
_____
_____
_____

My Favorite Dessert

Ingredients:

_____
_____
_____
_____
_____

Directions:

_____
_____
_____
_____
_____
_____
_____
_____

I've always been really good at

_____

_____

_____

_____

_____

_____

_____

_____

_____

_____

_____

_____

I was never very good at

_____

_____

_____

_____

_____

_____

_____

_____

_____

_____

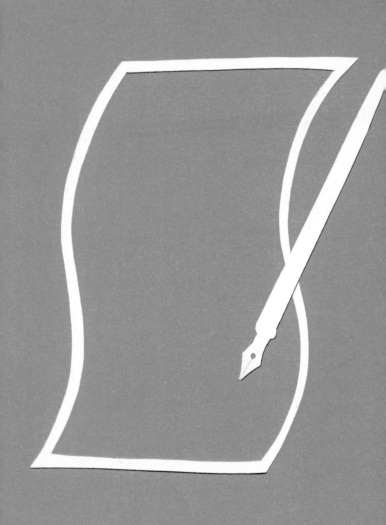

I became a Christian when I was

_____

The story goes

_____

_____

_____

_____

_____

_____

_____

_____

_____

_____

_____

_____

A major historical event that occurred in my lifetime was

Here's how it impacted me.

Is not wisdom found among the aged? Does not long life bring understanding?

THE BOOK OF JOB

Wisdom

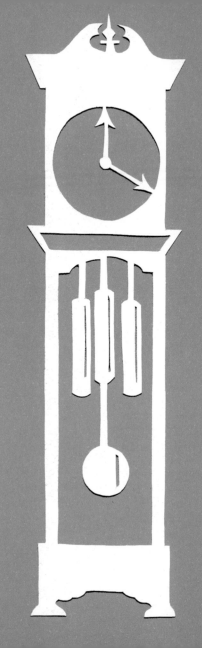

Something I wish I had learned earlier in life was

_____

_____

_____

_____

_____

_____

_____

_____

_____

_____

_____

_____

_____

I remember this time
when I overcame adversity.

I don't have many regrets,
but I would have loved to

The hardest thing
I've lived through was

What got me through was

My best marriage advice would be to

_____

_____

_____

_____

_____

_____

_____

_____

_____

_____

_____

_____

_____

_____

_____

_____

_____

My best parenting advice would be to

_____

_____

_____

_____

_____

_____

_____

_____

_____

_____

_____

_____

_____

_____

_____

The Lord is good and
his love endures forever;
his faithfulness continues
through all generations.

THE BOOK OF PSALMS

You & Me!

I love that you call me

(Grammy, Papa, Grams, etc.)

I like to call you

The first time I met you, I felt

If I could go anywhere in the
world with you, it would be

_____

_____

_____

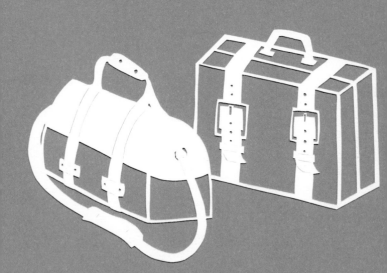

And we would

The day you were born, I was

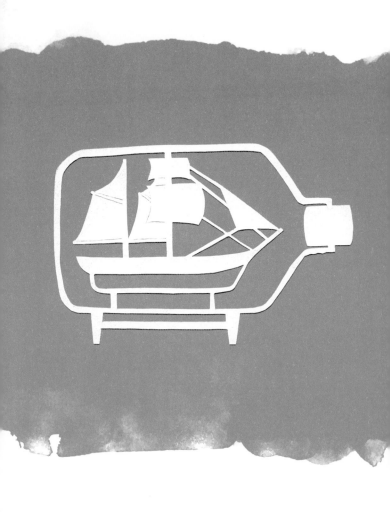

When you came to visit,
your favorite toy was

_____

_____

_____

_____

_____

I remember the time you and I laughed and laughed. Here's that story.

When you were little, I prayed over you.
I would ask God to

_____

_____

_____

_____

_____

_____

_____

_____

_____

_____

_____

_____

_____

We've had so many fun times together.
One of my favorite times was when we

_____

_____

_____

_____

_____

_____

_____

_____

_____

_____

_____

_____

_____

Here's the story of a time
you got into mischief.

The best part of being a grandparent is

I will pour out my Spirit on your offspring, and my blessing on your descendants.

THE BOOK OF ISAIAH